IT WORKS

SIMPLE KEYS

IT WORKS

With

SIMPLE KEYS™

R.H. Jarrett

Sumner M. Davenport

Self-Investment Company
2219 E. Thousand Oaks Blvd. #102-386
Thousand Oaks, Ca 91362

Graphics and Cover, Sumner M. Davenport © 2007
Research & Editing, Sumner M. Davenport © 2007
Published by Self-Investment Company, LLC © 2007

Manufactured in the United States of America

ISBN 10: 0-9815238-0-3
ISBN 13: 978-0-9815238-0-4

Over 1 million copies in print by 1926

Unlimited potential in 2007

An updated edition of

"It Works"

"**The Famous Little Red Book**

That Makes Your Dreams Come True"

now with **Simple Keys™** .

…If you KNOW what you *DESIRE*

You can HAVE it…

By R.H. Jarrett 1926
and
Sumner M. Davenport © 2007

Gratitude

*"Feeling gratitude and not expressing it
is like wrapping a present and not giving it."*
~ William Arthur Ward ~

First of all, my thanks to R.H. Jarrett for giving the world the original publication of **It Works.** Thank you to all the inspired "leaders" whose quotes are used throughout this book, and whose lives, works and words continue to inspire.

I thank my Source for everything in my life, my growth and my blessings. I thank all my teachers and guides, the sages and Angels in my daily life.

I thank my Grandpa, Everett Sumner Burbank, for many special times, magical moments, medicinal laughter and chats with Angels, and for continuing to be my spiritual guide.

I give heartfelt Gratitude to Whitney Challed for being all that a friend is, for being a safe harbor, laughing buddy, inspiration and for seeing my vision with me. Thank you to Gerrit Schroeder for providing connections and answers which added to the exciting journey of these books. I appreciate Marge Diehl for always seeing me as an Angel, for laughing with me. Thank you to Alan Diehl for being a quiet support at a special time of need. My world is blessed by Bryan Diehl for being proud of me even when I was having difficulty feeling proud of myself. Thank you to Mary Patterson for showing me a new insight to Faith and Spiritual beliefs. I feel inspired by Pat Patterson for always believing in the Common Wealth. For listening to what held a special place in my heart, I appreciate Mor Koren for my personalized custom pink gratitude book. Thank you to Joshua and Carter for lessons in childlike innocence and unconditional love.

My blessings are countless because of Duffy, Honey, Mattie, La Fleur, Rom, Luna, Wenchmore, Milo, Miko, Rufie, Sydney, Ashley, Blue, Chocolate, Angela and Crystal; all Angels in fur and feathers. And very special Gratitude to my constant furry companion Lancelot who teaches me that there is always a simple solution to everything and sometimes naps are necessary.

Thank you to Google™, Wikipedia and the Thousand Oaks Library, for helping me to find the quotes and the supporting information for this book.

Thank you to all the new readers of this book, and the changes you will make in your lives when you utilize the tools. And thank for the ripple effects from those new choices which will cause additional changes in the world for all of us.

It Works with Simple Keys

INTRODUCTION

Years ago a man wrote a book titled *It Works*. It was originally published in 1929, and is reported to have immediately risen to sales of over 1,000,000. It was a simple explanation of how to achieve your desires. Countless people followed the simple message and saw dramatic changes in their lives.

It Works presents a concise definite result-full plan for bettering your conditions in life. It shows you how to use the Mighty Power within yourself that is anxious and willing to serve you if you know how to use it.

It Works shows you how. All scientific, psychological and theological explanations are boiled down to ten minutes of interesting facts, a definite plan and ***three short rules of accomplishment.***

Some of the original examples have been updated in this book to fit more with today's times. However, humankind has not changed. We still have the same needs, desires, and dreams. In that truth, this information is timeless.

Have you ever noticed that a strategic planning book that is used in sports is referred to as a "playbook", and the planning books normally used to schedule and plan our lives is called a "workbook"?! Most people prefer to play rather than work, yet they spend the majority of their time *working* at life. This book is a strategic GUIDE. You can choose to make it playful or work.

Throughout this book the word "want" has been changed to "*desire*". To *want* something is to constantly be aware of not having it. The information in this book places a focus on your "***desires***" and the having of those desires.

More about how these words influence your energy, motivation and attainment are presented in the first

2

Simple Key DESIRE. When your creative energy is fully understood, the effects will seem to be almost miraculous.

You need not acquire this power, you already have it. However, you must you must be willing to understand it; you must use it you must take responsibility for it, so you can fully empower yourself with your creative energy.

Throughout the book you will read examples and references to what "many" or "most" people do with their desires and the journey towards them. Studies show that the majority of people exist without reaching their goals, and without having their desires met. They occasionally make an effort; they sporadically focus on what they want, spending more time complaining about what they do have or don't like. You will find answers and techniques throughout the original text of It Works and the Simple Keys so you can step apart from the majority and be a part of the group that lives the life of their dreams.

Everything that RHJ says in **"It Works"**, actually does work. However, in its simplicity, some people miss the depth of **The Plan**, leaving them with a few specific unanswered questions. Such as "How can I do this in my life?", "What can I do when I get frustrated or fall back into old habits?", or "Where do I find the support?"

Added to the original **It Works** text you will find nine Simple Keys™. These Keys are excerpts from the Simple Keys™ teachings. These keys support **The Plan** and the **Three Short Rules**. The Simple Keys™ provide tools, practices and explanations to assist you in understanding how to "fill in the blanks".

The information in this book is not new. My research shows it was first written about in Epictetus 360 AD, which was then translated in 1888. Many authors and educators have repeated the information in various formats over the years. This same information has been repeated over the decades.

INTRODUCTION

Some people will skim through and call this information *"interesting"*. Other people will say that they "already know this" and they "already do this".

"This is what learning is.
You suddenly understand something you've
understood all your life, but in a new way."
~ Doris Lessing ~

If you already have everything you desire, then continue what you are now doing.

On the other hand, if you are still meeting with disappointments and frustrations then this book may be offering you answers and techniques that could bring you new results.

Quotes from various authors and educators, past and present, which have inspired me throughout the years, are included within this book. They are all saying the same message, only in different words. They are each given a short introduction in the Quote References section of this book.

> *"Life is either a daring adventure*
> *or nothing."*
> *~ Helen Keller ~*

In order to gain the most benefit from this book, you must make a commitment to reading the entire book, **and** following the suggestions as they are presented.

If you will devote the minimum of 10 minutes every day as RHJ suggests, for only 21 days, you will see a difference in your life.

The timeless message of RHJ and the Simple Keys has been proven time and again.

INTRODUCTION

This information could have extended easily over 350 pages; however it has deliberately shortened to make it as easy as possible for you to read, understand and apply.

In several areas, writing space has been provided so you can make this book an active learning tool.

"One new perception, one fresh thought,
one act of surrender, one change of heart,
one leap of faith,
can change your life forever."
~ Robert Holden ~

Will you try it? Simply stated, thousands of bettered lives will testify to the fact that "**It Simply Works".**

The 3rd Edition of this book will be published with testimonials from readers who applied the tools and the results they saw. If you would like to submit your testimonial for consideration for inclusion in the 3rd Edition, please send your testimonial to the email address indicated in the Results section of this book.

"It's not that some people have willpower
and some don't.
It's that some people are ready to change
and others are not."
~ James Gordon, M.D. ~

I wish you a joyous abundant life.

SUMNER MICHAELS DAVENPORT
Co Author, Editor

INTRODUCTION

It Works with Simple Keys

Table of Contents

PREFACE

Do not let your worldly, incredulous objective mind keep you from more prosperity and happiness than you have dreamed of.

Test the power of this baffling book that defies tradition and experience. Thousands have tried the plan it presents and know in truth that *It does Work.*

> *"All who joy would win*
> *must share it,*
> *Happiness was born as twin."*
> *~ BYRON ~*

RHJ

It Works

JFS

*The author RHJ sent the manuscript of this book for criticism to a friend who returned it with the notation. **"It Works"**. This judgment born of experience was adopted as the title of the book – Publishers 1926.

The man who wrote this book in 1926 was a highly successful businessman, widely known for his generosity and helpful spirit. He gave full credit for all that he had accomplished in mastering circumstances, accumulating wealth and winning friends to the silent working out of the simple, powerful truth which he tells of in this work. He shows you here an easy, open road to a larger, happier life. Knowing that the greatest good comes from helping others without expecting praise, the original author of this work requested that his name be omitted when the book was first published. In later editions he was recognized as R.H. Jarrett.

 A concise, definite, result-full plan with rules, explanations and suggestions for bettering your condition in life.

...If you KNOW what you *DESIRE*
you can HAVE IT...

See Simple Key DESIRE

What is the real secret of obtaining
desirable possessions?

Are some people born under a lucky star or other charm which enables them to have all that which seems so desirable, and if not what is the cause of the difference in conditions under which men and women live?

Many years ago, feeling that there must be a logical answer to this question, I (RHJ) decided to find out, if possible what it was. I found the answer to my own satisfaction, and for years have given the information to others who have used it successfully.

From a scientific, psychological or theological viewpoint, some of the following statements may be interpreted as incorrect, but nevertheless, the plan has brought the results desired to those who have followed the simple instructions and it my sincere belief that I am now presenting it in a way which will bring happiness and possessions to many more.

"If wishes were horses, beggars would ride." Is the attitude taken by the average man and woman in regard to possessions. They are not aware of *a power* so near that it is overlooked; so simple in operation that it is difficult to conceive; and so sure in results that it is not made use of consciously, or recognized and *the cause of failure or success.*

"Wow, I wish that were mine", is the outburst of Jimmy, the fast food restaurant cashier as the new red Hummer goes by; and Debbie, the receptionist, expresses the same thought regarding a ring in the jeweler's window; while poor old Jones, the accountant, during the Sunday walk, replies to his wife, "Yes, dear, it would be nice to have a home like that, but it is out of the question. We will have to continue to rent." Erik, the salesman, protests that he does all the work, gets the short end of the money and will someday quit his job and find a real one, and President Alexander, in his private sanctorum, voices a bitter tirade against the annual attack of hay-fever.

At home, it is much the same. Last evening, David declared that his daughter Marianne was headed straight for disaster, and today, a single mother's limited income problem and other trying affairs fade into insignificance as she exclaims, "this is the last straw. Bobby's school teacher wants to see me this afternoon. His reports are terrible, I know, but I'm already late for my girl's night out. She'll have to wait until tomorrow."

So goes the endless stream of expressions like these from millions of people in all classes who give no thought to what they really *desire* and **who are getting all they are entitled to or expect**.

If you are one of these millions of thoughtless talkers or wishers and would like a decided change from your present condition, you can have it; but first of all, you must KNOW what you *desire* and this is no easy task for some.

When you can train your objective, conscious mind (the one you use everyday) to decide definitely upon the things or conditions you desire, you will have taken your first big step in accomplishing or securing what you know you *desire*.

To get what you *desire* is no more mysterious or uncertain that the stereo waves all around you.

Tune in correctly and you get a perfect result.

But to do this of course, it is necessary to know something of your equipment and have a plan of operation.

 See Simple Key LIFE CHANGING

You have within you a *mighty power*, anxious and willing to serve you, a power capable of giving you *that which you seriously desire*. This power is described by Thomas Jay Hudson, Ph.D., LL.D., and author of "The Law of Psychic Phenomena" as your *subjective mind.* Other educated and well-known authors use different names and *terms but all agree that it is omnipotent. (Unlimited; all powerful).* Therefore, I call this Power, "Emmanuel" (God in us).

Regardless of the name of this Great Power, or the conscious admission of God, the Power is *capable and willing* to carry to a complete a perfect conclusion every serious desire of your objective mind, but you must be really serious about what you *desire.* Occasional wishing or half-hearted thoughts do not form a perfect connection or communication with *your omnipotent (unlimited) power.* You must be serious, willing to make the commitment (to yourself) and *sincerely and truthfully* desiring certain conditions or things in your life – mental, physical or spiritual.

Your *objective mind and personal will are so wishy-washy that you usually only WISH for things and the wonderful, capable power within you does not function. Your <u>Wish</u> simply washes away in your next breath.*

Most wishes are simply just meaningless words. Jimmy, the fast food restaurant cashier gave no thought to actually having the red Hummer. Erik, the salesman, was not thinking of any other job or even thinking at all. President Alexander knew he had hay fever and was expecting it. David's business was quite likely successful and the single mother no doubt had fun with her friends, that day, but they had no fixed ideas of what they really *desired* for their children to accomplish and were actually helping to being about the same unhappy conditions which existed.

If you are really serious about changing your present condition, here is a *concise, definite, result-full plan, with rules, explanations and suggestions.*

It Works with Simple Keys

THE PLAN

Write down on paper in order of their importance, the things and conditions you really *desire*.

Do not be afraid of *desiring* too much. Go the limit in writing down your *desire*s.

 See Simple Key DESIRE

Change the *LIST* daily, adding to or taking away from it, until you have it about right.

Do not be discouraged on account of changes, as this is natural. There will always be changes and additions with accomplishments and increasing desires.

DESIRE

What Do You Really *Desire*?

Although this is the starting point, it is where many people stop.

In many religious cultures, a GOD is given all the credit for the results in life. In many spiritual practices, others accept that Universal Energy is the Omnipresent Power. Both are right. **GOD** = **G**enerates, **O**rchestrates and **D**elivers.

You are one with this creative power when you pray without ceasing, when you mindfully meditate, when you focus on your desires, commit to having them, open your willingness to clear your old internal instructions and messages from your mind, and create the space for your desires to take root and express gratitude for it all. You are also one with this power when you mindlessly go about your day complaining and thinking about what you don't have and don't like.

For years countless have been telling themselves, "they can't have", "can't afford", "can't be" and "shouldn't do". They have adopted the belief that other people can, and they can't. Their daily conversation is filled with more frustration of what they don't have, than talk of their dreams and desires.

Over the years many people have adopted the belief that "only dishonest people are rich", "no one in my family has ever achieved their dreams, so I can't either"; "I can't because I don't have the money, the education or the connections"; "my family is fat, so I will always be fat"; "it's a sin to *desire* material things"; "It would be wrong to make more money than my parents, or my spouse", and more….

"People are always blaming their circumstances
for where they are.
I don't believe in circumstances.
The people who get on in this world
are the people who get up and look for the
circumstances they desire.
And if they can't find them,
they make them."
~ George Bernard Shaw ~

Over the years many people have also developed feelings of unworthiness. These feelings come from a variety of experiences and choices. (More on worthiness in Simple Key **WHY NOT YOU?**)

*"Know that although in the eternal scheme of
things you are small, you are also unique and
irreplaceable, as are all your fellow humans
everywhere in the world."*

~ Margaret Laurence ~

Now is the time you can choose to keep your old thoughts, beliefs and excuses or accept that you CAN have anything you really *desire* when you are ready to follow The Plan and take the action required.

How many of your beliefs are your own? How many of your beliefs qualify as *"knowing" from a Personal experience"?*

*"Re-examine all you have been told.
Dismiss what insults your Soul."*

~ Walt Whitman ~

In order to re-train your beliefs in having what you *desire*, you must first know what you *desire*.

The words you use whether you talk silently to yourself or out loud have an effect on your energy and motivation. When your energy feels good, you feel good and you are more motivated to do something. Every word you think or speak is energy. This thought energy stimulates a feeling. Every feeling you have is energy and stimulates thoughts. It is an ever present cycle. Each word and feeling energy is stimulating and feeding the other. Every thought and feeling that you allowed to take root in your mind and body in the past is still with you, and is controlling you to think and do the same things. This includes your complaints, your aggravations, your judgments, your fears as well as your joys, your excitements, your pride, your confidence, and so on.

When a piano is played, someone places their fingers on the keys which then strike a chord against the strings which are rooted in the body of the piano. Whenever the same key is pressed, it will stimulate only the same string in the piano. If the piano was unappreciated and neglected or played harshly, it will change the sound resonating from the inner workings. The piano needs to be re-tuned to begin play its beautiful music again.

If you are working with a computer that has been given bad commands, this will interfere with its ability to function at its optimum level to create the results you require. You will need to re-program your computer and root its system in order to change the results it creates.

Similarly, when you focus on a desire of an accomplishment today, you may be striking old chords and old inner commands from the past that have taken root in your system. Thinking and doing the same things will always get you the same results. When you desire different results, you must consciously uproot and replace the old thoughts.

The following are three Simple Key techniques to assist you in clarifying what you *desire*.

Step #1:

OBSERVE & REPLACE

Have you ever had a feeling of being tired and having no energy to do anything, and then, a friend calls and asked you to do something fun, something you liked and wanted to do? Did your energy suddenly change? At that time you may not have been aware of the significance in your ability to make this shift.

In order to consciously uproot and replace the old thoughts and commands you must be consciously aware of the feelings you have associated with these thoughts. When referring to feelings I am suggesting more than simply happy or sad. Your thoughts and feelings are in several parts of your body. Once you are aware of the effect your words have on you and your motivation, you can make the conscious choice to re-train yourself in how you speak and think.

Practice the steps of this experiment to recognize your personal energy reaction to words:

Part 1a:

Tell yourself something you WANT in your life. Say "I want *(fill in the blank).*

Take notice of how you feel.

Are you breathing fully or shallow?

How does your solar plexus, your stomach area feel?

How does your back feel?

Do you feel comfortable or uncomfortable?

Where are your eyes focused?

Are you hot or cold?

Are you trembling or feeling solid?

Are you standing tall or slumping?

Write your perceptions here:

Simple Key - DESIRE

Before you start this next part, stand up and take a very deep breath and let it out.

Part 1b:

Now tell yourself the same something using *Desire* instead of Want. Say "I **desire** *(fill in the blank).*

Take notice of how you feel.

Are you feeling the same or different?

Are you breathing fully or shallow?

How does your solar plexus, your stomach area feel?

How does your back feel?

Do you feel comfortable or uncomfortable?

Are you hot or cold?

Are you trembling or feeling solid?

Are you breathing fully or shallow?

Are you standing tall or slumping?

Write your perceptions here:

It Works with Simple Keys

Most people will find a distinct difference when they state their Desire. They feel lighter, they stand taller, their breathing is smoother and relaxed, they feel more comfortable, their eyes are focused in front of themselves, and many times they feel a little excited. Others may need to do this simple experiment a second time or at a later date when they are in the mood, relaxed and able to recognize the differences.

You can use this same experiment with the words: "work" and "play".

Part 2a:

Tell yourself. "Life is such work"; or "relationships are such work"; or "making money is such work".

Take notice of how you feel.

Are you breathing fully or shallow?

How does your solar plexus, your stomach area feel?

How does your back feel?

Do you feel comfortable or uncomfortable?

Are you hot or cold?

Are you trembling or feeling solid?

Are you breathing fully or shallow?

Are you standing tall or slumping?

Write your perceptions here:

Simple Key - DESIRE

Before you start the next part, stand up and take a very deep breath and let it out.

Part 2b:

Now replace the word: work: with the words "playful and easy". "Life is so playful and easy"; or "relationships are so "playful and easy"; or "making money is so "playful and easy".

Take notice of how you feel.

Are you feeling the same or different?

Are you breathing fully or shallow?

How does your solar plexus, your stomach area feel?

How does your back feel?

Do you feel comfortable or uncomfortable?

Are you hot or cold?

Are you trembling or feeling solid?

Are you breathing fully or shallow?

Are you standing tall or slumping?

Write your perceptions here:

It Works with Simple Keys

At some point in our lives, most people were told and conditioned to believe that "work" meant difficulty, potentially painful, sacrifice, struggle and limited rewards.

Until you recondition your belief about the word "work", you need to replace it.

Choose a word that reflects the truth about your desires. Be careful with simply using any word, or a word substitute that feels the same as the word you are seeking to replace.

As an example, some people have used the words "challenge" or "opportunity" to replace the word "problem". Unfortunately, the words "challenge" and "opportunity" many times will carry the same energy and feel the same as the word "problem".

Many people find the words "playful", "easy" and "effortless" fit very easily when talking about their desires. Test your choice of words until you find ones that fit for you.

What are your chosen replacement words? List them here.

Take notice of how you feel. Next to each word write how you feel.

Are you breathing fully or shallow?

How does your solar plexus, your stomach area feel?

How does your back feel?

Do you feel comfortable or uncomfortable?

Are you hot or cold?

Are you trembling or feeling solid?

Are you breathing fully or shallow?

Are you standing tall or slumping?

Test your choice of words until you find ones that stimulate the feelings in you that you desire.

Start here:

Simple Key - DESIRE

Step #2:

REPHRASE & OBSERVE

What are you saying to yourself and others about what you don't *want*? "I don't *want* to be broke"; "I don't *want* to be fat"; "I don't *want*.....etc.

(a) Stop and **Rephrase** each sentence to state exactly the opposite: "I *desire* to be wealthy"; "I *desire* to be thin and healthy"; "I *desire*.....etc...

Write each re-phrase six (6) times for each statement.

(b) Now start a clean list. Write down only your **"I Desire"** statements.

This is the *LIST* that RHJ describes in *The Plan*.

Start Here:

Simple Key - DESIRE

You may find that as you write your "*I Desires*", your mind will start chattering some of the reasons why you can't. These are all the old messages you have been holding on to, and living your life by.

If this happens, many people will try to fight back the thought. Remember the old joke about the pink elephant? You were told that under no conditions are you to think about a pink elephant. So do NOT think about the pink elephant. What happens? All you can think about is the pink elephant!

Other people will say the word "erase" when one of these old messages looms in. The problem with focusing on erase is that you are still focusing on what you are trying to erase. It's time to use a new technique.

I had been taught by therapists, workshop leaders and the many books that I had read the importance of getting these feelings out by writing them down. But what was the most effective way to do it? And when I did write out these thoughts, then what?!

One day when I was feeling overwhelmed and haunted again by old memories of a painful experience and feeling angry and helpless, I suddenly felt guided to write everything out, letting the emotions flow as well. It was during this writing experience that it also "came to me" to then OVERWRITE these words with statements of strength and worthiness. It seemed like a simple solution and I was willing to try anything at that point in my pain.

I felt guided to begin writing in pencil instead of pen as I had done in the past. I wrote all my feelings, all my pain and all my anger. Even though I was exhausted from my writings, with only a small amount of strength to continue, I was determined. I then wrote BOLD statements of "I am capable, worthy, smart, etc" and "I can do, be and have", as well as other reinforcing statements of receiving and accomplishing my desires. I wrote how great it felt to have, to be and to accomplish.

As I wrote and re-read my BOLD statements I began to feel the difference in my body, my breathing and my emotions. From a feeling of helplessness, I was now beginning to feel empowered and hopeful.

My bold statements became declarations, overwriting the pencil written words so well, that the old messages faded.

Your pencil writings will fade under the weight of the black felt tip ink when you follow this same technique.

Take out a single piece of paper. Using a dull PENCIL begin writing down those thoughts, statements and old messages that are running through your mind as you start to focus on your desires.

Write down all of those reasons and excuses that you have listened to so many times in the past, those messages you have heard echo in your mind for so long that you mistakenly believe they are the truth.

Keep writing as fast as you can.

When the paper appears full, turn it upside down, same side up and keep writing. Now you are writing over your previously written sentences.

Keep writing every reason why you "can't have". "can't be", all the "should's" and "should not's". Let your handwriting be sloppy, let your grammar be whatever it is and keep writing.

When the page appears full again, turn the page sideways and keep writing. Same side of the paper. Keep writing until these thoughts run out.

If you have never used this technique in the past, it may seem like a long process. Keep your commitment to your desires and keep writing and emptying these words onto the paper. It is important to empty your mind so you can start clean.

When your mind is done chattering, put down the pencil and pick up a dark, thick BLACK FELT TIP PEN.

Start at the top of this page, and using your BLACK FELT TIP PEN, start writing your "*I desires*" completely over the pencil writings. Write larger and bolder with your black felt tip pen.

When you use your black felt tip pen to write over the top of your previous pencil statement, the pencil writings will fade in the background, and the black pen statements will become predominant on the page. This way, all you can see when you are done, is WHAT YOU DESIRE – **BOLDLY!**

Continue writing your BOLD declarations until the page is full, then take out another piece of clean paper and keep writing. Or start writing these Bold statements into a personal journal. Fill both sides of the sheets of clean paper. Use as many pieces of paper as necessary. Keep writing until all you can think about is what you are writing in **Bold Black ink.**

When you are finished, you will have pages of strong bold declarations. You can keep the loose pages of bold statements in a binder, or re-read your journal of bold statements, to remind you. Your pencil page with bold overwriting is part of your healing and release, so you can dispose of this page.

After doing this writing and release, it is important to get up and move your body around. Put on music you enjoy and move to it, or take a short walk, or shake out your arms and legs. Find the physical release that works for you.

This is one powerful method of re-phrasing and re-training your conscious and subconscious mind. This is redirecting your focus onto what you *DESIRE*.

Some people will chant affirmations without first cleaning out the old chatter. This can be compared to putting clean water into glass already filled with dirty water. If you keep the clean water running long enough, eventually the dirty water will become more and clearer. On the other hand, emptying the dirty water out of the glass first before putting in clean water will make it easier and faster to have a glass full of clean water. If you leave the water in the glass alone to sit undisturbed and with no clean water coming in, it will become stagnant again from the residual "dirt" in the original dirty glass or it can pick up dirt from outside influences. You must keep the clean flow of water going in to continually clean out the dirt. The same is true for your mind. You must use this technique EVERY TIME any of these old messages pop back into your mind.

Thoughts and verbal statements of "don't" and "can't" will continue to keep you from getting what you *desire*, keep you stuck and keep you where you have been.

Every time you re-phrase from **"Don't want"** ⇒ **to** ⇒ **"Desire",** you are shifting your focus onto what you desire. You are reinforcing your worthiness. You are opening your mind to possibilities and creative thinking.

"Whatever a person's mind dwells on intensely
and with firm resolve,
that is exactly what they become."
~ Shankaracharya ~

It is important to **re-phrase every time** you think or speak opposite of what you *DESIRE*, until the only thoughts that you hear and express are your BOLD declarations and your words and thoughts support you in what you *DESIRE*.

Step #3:

BE AWARE OF ROUTINE INFLUENCES

When you commit to making a change in your life, by focusing on your desires and dedicating yourself to having them, you must also be aware of the routine influences in your life.

What music do you listen to? When you listen, how do you feel? What words echo in your mind?

If you are tempted to say "its only words, no big deal". Think about this: If someone called you stupid, ugly or fat or slanderous and insulting words against your character, or worse – would they only be words?

Words have power over you - or words can work for you.

What movies and TV shows do you watch? What games do you play? What books and magazines do you read?

All of these routine influences have messages that either support you in staying where you are, or assist you in moving forward towards your desires.

Step #4:

GIVE YOUR FOCUS A BOOST

(a) Buy an upscale magazine such as Robb Report, High Performance Auto, Travel & Leisure and Lifestyles and look at the pictures.

(b) Cut out the pictures of those things you would like to have in your life. As you look through the magazines, if you find yourself saying that you don't *desire* something, immediately find something that you would like to have. This again, is re-focusing and re-training yourself to think in **DESIRES** instead of "don't wants", and I **CAN** instead of "can'ts".

(c) Once you have ideas of what you desire, start writing your *LIST* as RHJ stated in *The Plan*. Next to each item, place a photograph or cutout from the magazine wherever possible.

As you collect pages and *LISTS* of what you desire, you may find it useful to put them in a binder, or tape them to poster boards, so you can see them. Have you ever browsed through a store catalog and saw things that you liked and would like to have? You are creating your catalog; your own "Personal Self-Gift Catalog".

"Developing a prototype early
is the number one goal for our designers or
anyone else who has an idea, for that matter.
We don't trust it
until we can see it and feel it."
~ Win Ng ~

Make sure you are writing what you "specifically" *desire* on your *LIST*. How much money do you *desire*? What exact body weight and measurements do you *desire*? What size and style of home do you *desire*? In what city or neighborhood do you desire to live? What kind of car do you *desire*? Where do you *desire* to take your vacation?

You must be very specific with each one of these, as RHJ states in *The Three Positive Rules of Accomplishment.*

Years ago Jim Carrey, the actor, was heard on a talk show telling how he made a check payable to himself for $10 million dollars from a "studio" as payment for a film, when at the time he had barely enough to pay his rent. He looked at that $10 million dollar "payment" every day, and told himself he was worth $10 million dollars to be in a movie. Today, he is paid much more than that.

The authors of the Chicken Soup for the Soul books *desired* to have their books on the Best Seller booklist. In the beginning, before anyone really knew of them and their books, they took a copy of the Best Seller booklist and wrote their title in the number one line. Today they have hundreds of Chicken Soup titles, and many of them stay on the Best Seller lists longer than any other titles by other authors.

Be as specific as you can right now. As you find yourself thinking with more specifics, update your *LIST*. You may find your "*LIST*" actually turns into several paragraphs or bullet points.

Do not concern yourself at this point how any of this is going to be manifest or delivered to you. This step is to clarify for yourself what you *DESIRE*.

> *"Take the first step in faith.*
> *You don't have to see the whole staircase,*
> *just take the first step."*
> *~ Martin Luther King, Jr ~*

Start Here:

Simple Key - DESIRE

LIFE CHANGING

As you start to focus on what you *desire*, and as you begin to reach your goals and receive your *desires* – YOU WILL CHANGE!

> *"Things do not change;*
> *we change."*
> *~ Henry David Thoreau ~*

This is another time that just when things are beginning to happen, many people stop themselves.

"Without accepting the fact
that everything changes,
we cannot find perfect composure.
But unfortunately, although it is true, it is
difficult for us to accept it. Until we accept
the truth of transience, we suffer."
~ Shinichi Suzuki ~

If having more money is on your *LIST*, you will change – you will find yourself with more ease of spending as your money increases. You will begin to think and act with more confidence in receiving the money on your *LIST*, and more. You will begin to focus on having even more money, and watching for the opportunities that will bring it to you.

If having a healthier or slimmer body is on your *LIST*, you will change – you will find your self-image will change as your body changes. You will find your body changing as your self image changes.

If more "things" are on your *LIST*, you will change – you will find yourself enjoying the things you already have, the new things you get, and your *LIST* will grow with more *DESIRES*.

As you start to receive the desires on your *LIST*, you will begin to raise the level of your requests. Your faith and self confidence will increase. You will complain less and watch your words more carefully.

People will notice.

Some will admire you, some will criticize.

"When you rise above the masses you will always become a target. Just as a flower grows taller than the surrounding grass, and becomes a target for the nourishing sunshine, it also becomes a target to be cut down."
~ Sumner Davenport ~

In a conversation with a friend one day, when asked how I was as I moving through a problem that came into my life, I replied that I was focusing on solutions. She responded that she would do the same but since everyone else was complaining about everything, she felt she wouldn't fit unless she did the same.

*You need to ask yourself "**Which is more important – fitting in or having the life you desire?**"*

"The definition of Insanity is doing the same things and expecting different results."

~ Albert Einstein ~

When you start focusing on your DESIRES, and you start to have them and accomplish them, you will not longer "fit in" with the people who choose to focus on the problems and the excuses. Only you can decide if you want to fit in with the people who criticize and complain, or fit in with the group of people who are having and accomplishing their deepest DESIRES.

As you write your *LIST* of *DESIRES*, answer these two questions with each one:

How will I change?
How will this change my life?

Be deeply honest with yourself. Will you feel more freedom? Will you feel happier? Will you be more generous? Will you be afraid of what others will think and say? Will you be nice or mean?

Some people stop themselves because they are afraid of actually having what they really *DESIRE*; others are afraid of becoming "like those mean or dishonest people"; others are afraid people may not like them.

Make an agreement with yourself how you will grow in a positive way.

When you write how you will change next to your *DESIRES*, you will be reinforcing your positive change every time you read your *LIST*.

Start Here:

It Works with Simple Keys

3 Positive Rules of

Accomplishment

1. *Read your LIST of what you DESIRE **three times each day**: morning, noon and night*

TUNE IN

Now that you have identified your *DESIRES*, written a detailed *LIST*, collected pictures, and identified how your life will change, you have taken the first necessary action steps towards having your *DESIRES*.

This is usually another common place where many people stop. They write their *LIST*, look at a few pictures and then put their feet up, sip coffee and wait for someone to drop it at their doorstep.

"Your vision will become clear only

when you look into your heart.

Who looks outside, dreams.

Who looks inside, awakens."

~ Carl Jung ~

As RHJ explains in *The Plan*, you **must** read your *LIST* three times every day. If you have placed your *DESIRES* in a binder or on poster boards that make it difficult to carry with you, then also write your *LIST* on a paper that you can carry with you, so you can read it at any time, regardless of your whereabouts.

Many people give an occasional thought to what they *desire*. When you read your *LIST*, you must do more than simply read the words. You must dedicate yourself to "pray without ceasing", you must mindfully meditate, you must be focused, you must pay attention to your own thoughts and actions and you must believe that you already have what you are asking for and you must *listen* and watch for "Inspired Action" for you to take.

See Simple Key INSPIRED ACTION

"I've discovered that numerous peak
performers use the skill
of mental rehearsal of visualization.
They mentally run through important events
before they happen."
~ Charles A. Garfield ~

One of the most powerful ways to *Tune In* to your creative energy is with silent and sitting still "mindful meditative visualization". Once you have mastered sitting still mindful meditative visualization, you can then use your mindful meditative visualization power throughout your day.

You can teach yourself this "mindful meditative visualization" by doing the following three steps in the order presented. It is important to master each step before proceeding to the next. As you master each step you will notice your ability to master the step which follows, will become easier.

Step 1:

(a) Select a room where you can be alone and undisturbed; sit erect, and comfortable. It is important to keep your posture open and comfortable, to support your breathing.

(b) Close your eyes and breathe easy deep, comfortable breaths.

(c) Inhale deeply; and as you exhale, let your body relax; let go, let your muscles take their normal condition with your proper posture. This will remove all pressure from your nerves, and eliminate that tension which so frequently produces physical exhaustion.

Physical relaxation is a voluntary exercise of your will and this relaxation during your mindful meditative visualization will be found to be of great value, as it enables your blood to circulate freely to and from your brain and body.

Tensions lead to mental unrest and abnormal mental activity of your mind. It produces worry, care, fear and anxiety. Relaxation is therefore an absolute necessity in order to allow your mental faculties to exercise its greatest freedom.

Make this exercise as thorough and complete as possible, mentally determine that you will relax every muscle and nerve, until you feel quiet and restful and at peace yet awake and aware.

If you fall asleep during this exercise, it is an indication that you need more rest. It is important that you stay awake and aware.

(d) Staying awake and aware, let your thoughts roam where they will.

(e) Be perfectly still for from 5 minutes to fifteen minutes. The longer you can sit perfectly still, the better.

(f) Continue to practice this for three or four days or for a week until you can sit perfectly still for a minimum of 15 minutes.

Sitting perfectly still means no movement, no re-adjustment, scratching, fidgeting, or blinking. It is important to remember to breathe, so the movement of your chest or your diaphragm expanding is movement you will allow. Breathing is essential ☺

When you have mastered sitting perfectly still and relaxed, awake and aware, for 15 minutes, you a ready to proceed to step 2:

Step 2:

This time you will begin to control your thought. If possible always take the same room, the same chair, and the same position as you did for the previous step.

(a) Sit still, relaxed, awake and aware, as before, however, this time **STOP all thought.** This step will give you control over all thoughts of care, worry and fear, and will enable you to entertain only the kind of thoughts you desire.

For most people this is very difficult. The first time they do this they find themselves thinking "STOP thinking!"; "Why am I thinking"; "Why is that on my mind?"; "Can I do this?" and myriads of other thoughts.

*"Little by little, through patience
and repeated effort, the mind will become
stilled in the Self."*
~ Bhagavad Gita ~

This first part of this second step is valuable, because it is a very practical demonstration of the great number of thoughts which are constantly trying to gain access to your mental world. In order to keep the thoughts on what you *DESIRE* in your mind, you must make space.

It is a fact that no two things or thoughts, can occupy the exact same space at the exact same time.

Try it. One will either be on top or beside; before or after the other. If you attempt to force two things into the same exact space, they may end up merging into one. So, again, only one is occupying the space.

After you have done part (a) of this step and experienced the effort required to control your thoughts, you can use the following key to assist you in clearing your mind of all thoughts. By clearing your mind of all thoughts you can then begin choose which ones you *desire* to entertain when you meditate.

(b) Sit perfectly still, relaxed, awake and aware, as you have mastered in Step One, however, this time when you close your eyes, visualize a movie screen in your mind. See this screen and all the space around it, everything become the color solid Black.

(c) Once you are able to see only Black, then place and see a large white dot in the middle of the blackness.

(d) Focus on the white dot. Again, STOP all thought. Anytime a thought comes into your mind, go back to your focus on the white dot. Initially, you will find you are not able to do this for more that a few moments at a time.

(e) Continue practicing this step until you are able to master control over your thoughts. When you have accomplished this, proceed to step 3.

🗝 Step 3:

In this step you will be doing two things: you will be visualizing and listening.

You will be visualizing what you *DESIRE*, seeing yourself already in possession of whatever it is and LISTENING to your thoughts, and LISTENING for answers and guidance.

> *"Learn to pause...*
> *or nothing worthwhile*
> *will catch up to you."*
> *~ Doug King ~*

Every part of this third step should be practiced with ease. When you have mastered the two preceding steps, this step will be easy and powerful.

It is important that you have taken the time to write your *LIST* with specific *DESIRES*, and collected pictures of these things. The pictures you collect are to assist you in visualizing. What you see with your eyes open, you can duplicate with your eyes closed.

(a) Sit perfectly still, relaxed, awake and aware, as you have mastered.

(b) Close your eyes, visualize your movie screen in your mind with the big white dot in the middle of the blackness.

(c) Visualize in full color and action what you *DESIRE*; those things you have written on your *LIST*.

Project these images on the white dot on movie screen in your mind..

"All persons dream; but not equally.

Those who dream by night in the dusty

recesses of their minds wake in the day to

find that it was vanity: but the dreamers of

the day are dangerous people, for they may

act their dreams with open eyes,

to make it possible."

~ T.E. Lawrence ~

You **must** be seeing through your own eyes in your mind's picture.

If a certain amount of money is on your *LIST*, see through your eyes, you handing the bank teller your deposit. See your client handing you a signed order; see your hands opening an envelope with a check payable to you.

If a certain body image is on your *LIST*, see yourself looking at yourself in a mirror with the body look you *desire*.

If what you *desire* is a vacation at a certain place, see though your eyes this location. Continue to focus on your image until you can hear the sounds in your mind's ear, and smell the fragrances in your mind's nostrils.

The key is to see the picture vividly real on your mind's movie screen.

"If you don't know where you are going, then

how will you get there?

VISUALIZE !

Make pictures in your mind.

See the destination. Imagine your arrival.

Dream in perfect detail.

See yourself the way you desire to be when

you arrive. See yourself arriving.

*Make yourself a road map and study it every
day until you know the way
and the destination by heart."
~ Bryce Courtenay ~*

You must be able to feel as if you already have it.
This is a feeling of confidence, a knowing, a feeling of
excitement and a feeling of gratitude.

Your commitment to read your list three times every
day is very important, and will be what makes the
difference in your accomplishments and attainments.

Most people make sure they eat food at least three
times every day. They are conditioned to eat breakfast in
the morning, lunch at mid day, and dinner at the end of
the day and yet neglect to feed and recondition their
mind with nourishing thoughts and visions.

What if 15 minutes a day could actually make a
difference in having what you desire in your life? Would

it be worth the effort? Would it be worth changing your habits and exchanging old habits for new ones?

Reading your list at least three times a day can be as easy and nourishing as your regular daily meals.

3 Positive Rules of

Accomplishment - con't

#2. Think about what you desire as often as possible. If you find yourself thinking it can't be done, or you can't have it, you must go back to simply thinking about your LIST and what it is that you DESIRE.

Revisit Simple Ke y - DESIRE

FRUSTRATION BUMP

Most people will find times of frustration and struggle as they begin a new focus on their desires. This is the time to apply Step 2 of RHJ's instruction in "It Works" from the previous section.

When you focus on your desires and focus on having what is on your *list*, you will find more ease in changing your old habits for new habits.

Anytime you start to feel doubt, or hear yourself saying "can't have" or "can't do this", immediately pick up your list and start reading and envisioning.

Years ago I met a wonderful woman, Vetura Papke, who taught this a very important principle, and she called it the Golden Key to getting over your frustration bump.

In conversation with her one day, I asked what to do when things seemed to be going wrong. She replied that I should practice the Golden Key and refocus.

I retorted, "But what if things **really** seem to be going wrong?" She simply answered, "that is the time to **really** practice the Golden Key and refocus on your desires."

Simply put, the Golden Key is to move your focus, your thoughts and actions from the frustrating event, and place all your energy and focus back onto your desired reality.

When you change the focus of your energy, whatever you are experiencing at that time will change.

This is not some magical game nor is it simply daydreaming or wishing. It is the shifting of your energy.

If you continue to place your energy and focus on the struggle, you will continue to struggle.

When you shift your energy to your desired reality, you will find your body more relaxed, your thinking becomes clearer and you may receive inspired guidance of a solution.

3 Positive Rules of
Accomplishment - con't

#3. *Do **not** talk to any one about your plan except to the Great Power within you which will unfold to your Objective Mind the method of accomplishment.*

SUPPORT

"Keep away from people who try to belittle

your ambitions. Small people always do that,

but the really great people make you feel that

you too can become great."

~ Mark Twain ~

RHJ advises "not talk to any one about your plan except to the Great Power within you."

Sometimes even your most loving friends and family can be your greatest detractors. Some people will attempt to divert you "for your own good". Others may feel they have better advice or know better how you should be living your life. To have what YOU desire, it is important to heed the words of RHJ.

One day while having coffee with a young lady she was talking about her LIST. She went on to say, that she was telling her friends what was on her LIST and how she was following *The Plan*, "because they were 100% supportive in her having what she *desired*." Just then two of her well-meaning friends happened by the table. The young lady I was talking with spoke to her friends and asked them to tell me how they were 100% supportive of her *desires*. They both said "Yes, of course." Then one went on to say, "Well, in order for her to really have what she *desires*, she has to do this and that..." and then the other friend chimed in and said "And she needs to change this and that or it will never happen". So her 100% supportive friends actually believed that she could only have her *desires* if she changed according to the way they believed. (This and that were specific examples relating to the young lady's *desires*.)

When looking for people to support you in having your *desires*, look for people who are following the same Plan that you are. Find a mentor or master-mind group.

Walt Disney wasn't the typical Hollywood mogul. Instead of socializing with the "who's who" of the Hollywood entertainment industry, he would stay home and have dinner with his wife, Lillian, and his daughters, Diane and Sharon. In fact, socializing was a bit boring to Walt Disney. The people that where close to Walt were those who lived with him and his ideas, or both.

"Don't wait.
The time will never be just right."
~ Napoleon Hill~

3 Positive Rules of
Accomplishment - con't

It is obvious that you can not acquire faith at the start. Some of your *desires,* from all practical reasoning, may seem positively unattainable; but, nevertheless, write them down on your *LIST* in the proper place of important to you.

There is no need to analyze how this Power within you is going to accomplish your *DESIRES*. Such a procedure is a unnecessary as trying to figure out why a grain of corn placed in fertile soil shoots up a green stalk, blossoms and produces an ear of corn containing hundreds of grains, each capable of doing what the one grain did.

If you will follow this definite plan and carry out the three simple rules, the method of accomplishment will unfurl quite as mysteriously as the ear of corn appears on the stalk, and in most case much sooner than you expect.

When new *DESIRES* deserving position at or about the top of your *LIST*, come to you, then you may rest assured you are progressing correctly.

When you start removing from your *LIST* items which at first you thought you *DESIRED*, this **is another sure indication of progress.**

It is natural to be skeptical and have doubts, distrust and questionings, but when these thoughts arise, get out your LIST. Read it over; or if you have it memorized, talk to your inner self about your desires until the doubts that interfere with your progress are gone.

Remember, nothing can prevent you from having that which you seriously desire. *Others have these things.* **Why not you?**

WHY NOT YOU?!

"What you are accomplishing

may seem like a drop in the ocean.

But if this drop were not in the ocean,

it would be missed."

~ Mother Theresa ~

Have you ever heard yourself say" *I can't because......"*

    (a) .....I don't have the education, or I'm not smart enough.

    (b) .....I don't have the money.

    (c) .....I've always failed in the past.

(d) .....I don't know how it will be done.

(e) .....I don't have the time.

(f) .....I don't......

(a) If you said .....
I don't have the education,
or I'm not smart enough.

"Knowledge is of two kinds:
we know a subject ourselves,
or we know where we can find
information upon it."
~Samuel Johnson~

Henry Ford had a long and prosperous career manufacturing automobiles. He personally did not know how to build one, so instead of killing his dream, he found other people who had the knowledge and skills.

He surrounded himself with the people who could build his dream cars.

Do you need a more current example?: Les Brown, Successful Entrepreneur, Best Selling Author, Radio and Television Celebrity has had no formal education beyond high school, but with persistence and determination he has initiated and continued a process of unending self-education which has distinguished him as an authority on harnessing human potential. Les Brown's passion to learn and his hunger to realize greatness in himself and others helped him to achieve greatness.

And sometimes admitting to not knowing all the answers is your perfect place to start.

"It is impossible for a person to learn what they think they already know."

~ Epictetus ~

"The dumbest people I know
are those who know it all."
~ Malcolm Forbes ~

(b) If you said ....
I don't have the money.

Many people give up on what they *DESIRE* because they believe a certain amount of money is **necessary** for its attainment and it is impossible otherwise. By focusing on money as the obstacle to having, you will miss opportunities for support, answers and other creative solutions.

If your *LIST* includes a thing, such as a car, there are many ways to get a new car without spending a great deal of money, and sometimes no money. Some people go to work for companies that provide new cars for their employees; some people become test drivers for company's new cars; some people enter contests and involve themselves in projects where a car is the reward.

There are companies that hire people to housesit fine homes and drive the homeowner's vehicles while the owners are on extended vacations. For other things, mystery shoppers get paid to try products and services.

If your *LIST* includes attractive clothing, you may find local manufacturers in your area desiring to sell their "sample" display clothes.

Years ago, I met a man who *desire*d to own a clothing store, and didn't have the funds that he believed were required. He started visiting the Los Angeles Clothing Mart, buying the "samples" and "sales display" items for greatly reduced prices with whatever amount of money he could scrape together.

He then took these purchases to local swap meets and sold them for a little more than he paid for them. He then took this money back to the Mart and bought more clothes. Then back to the swap meet. He did this over and over again; until he had the amount he thought he needed to open a retail store. In the process however, he discovered that he really enjoyed the benefits of his current work schedule of one day at the clothing mart and two days at the swap meet. So instead of opening a retail store in one location, he continued what he was already doing, only on a bigger scale. He now has other people working for him at various swap meets and he spends his time overseeing a very flexible business.

Two other people however, *desired* to provide internet service for less, in fact, they *desired* to provide it for free.* They wrote a compelling business plan and showing it to a number of investors, were promptly turned down by all of them. Finally one enterprising investment company saw the potential in their business plan, and provided the financial backing NetZero needed to get started. (*When Net Zero was first introduced they offered internet access for free.)

(c) If you said …
I've always failed in the past.

"I never failed once.
It just happened to be a 2000-step process."
~ Thomas Edison ~

Walt Disney had a passionate *desire* to pursue a career in commercial art, which is how he began his original experiments in animation. He started by producing short animated films for local businesses in Kansas City. By the time Walt had started to create *The Alice Comedies*, which was about a real girl and her adventures in an animated world, he ran out of money. His company at the time. Laugh-O-Grams went bankrupt.

Instead of giving up, Walt packed his suitcase and with his unfinished print of *The Alice Comedies* in hand, headed for Hollywood to start a new business. It was Walt Disney's enthusiasm and faith in himself and others that took him straight to the top of Hollywood society. Walt Disney's dream of a clean and organized amusement park also came true when Disneyland Park in Anaheim opened in 1955.

Wally Amos opened his first Famous Amos store, with cookies based on his aunt's recipe which he baked himself. Within 10 years his sales had grown to more than $10 million. Due to financial troubles, Amos was forced to sell the Famous Amos Company, and trademarked name "Famous Amos".

Turning adversity into opportunity, Amos launched a new cookie venture, The Uncle Noname's Cookie Company. With America's tastes shifting towards healthier foods, the company focused on fat-free, nutritious muffins at that time. Uncle Noname ultimately became Uncle Wally's Muffin Company in 1999. The muffins are sold in more than 3,500 stores nationwide.

Dr. Seuss' first book was rejected by over 27 publishers. He had a fleeting thought to burn the manuscript. Instead he sent it out one more time.

The authors of Chicken Soup for the Soul were told by numerous publishers that "the title was too stupid" and that their book was "too positive".

What if you get a different result than you are asking for on your list? When this happens, many people will mistakenly think they are doing something wrong, or worse – that the are wrong; or they can't have what they are asking for or other destructive thoughts. Every result either takes you directly closer to your DESIRES, or it has an answer for your next step.

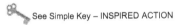 See Simple Key – INSPIRED ACTION

"Many of life's failures are people who did not
realize how close they were to success
when they gave up."
~ Thomas Edison ~

There are many true stories of how so many successful people have experienced failure and how they bounced back. To help you motivate yourself through your own failures try these three next simple steps:

Step #1:

Start researching successful people that you know or have heard about. Start with those people that YOU admire.

Read the biographies of these successful people. If they are still alive, find a way to interview them. Find out the details of their journey, especially the details of how they transformed any failure into the next step towards their success.

This is especially helpful when you find someone who has experienced similar challenges as you have.

Start your list here of people you will research:

"Whether you think that you can,

or that you can't, you are right."

~ Henry Ford ~

Step #2:

(a) Make a *LIST* of those projects you have started and completed successfully.

Start Here:

(b) Make a *LIST* of those times you exceeded your own expectations.

Start Here:

(c) Make a *LIST* of those things you have REALLY *desired* in the past, and you received

Start Here:

Step #3:

Find and learn from a mentor(s).

"Don't wait for someone to take you under their wing.
Find a wing to crawl under."
~ Dave Thomas ~

Successful people do not have conflict in their lives; they may actually have more, due to the level of their success. They have learned how to use it to their advantage. One of the best ways to learn how to be successful at anything is to surround yourself with people who are already successful and willing to share their information with you.

Find someone who is successful in their business, or in the business you *desire* to be in and ask if they will mentor you. Many successful people find it a compliment to be asked.

Some of the questions to ask yourself when seeking a mentor:

(1) Why have I selected this person?

(2) What do I already know about this person and their success and failures?

(3) What benefit is it to this person to be my Mentor? What can you offer this person in exchange for being your mentor? What is in it for the Mentor? Some Mentors will require you to prove your commitment and may give you a project to complete, or an accountability plan to follow. Some may require that you pay them for their time or donate to a charity they support. Be prepared to know what you have to offer. Before you say "I have nothing to offer", STOP, and think about it. Every person has something to offer.

(4) What do I expect to receive from this Mentor?

(5) What do I expect to achieve from working with this Mentor?

Step #4:

Surround yourself with like-minded people, Do your research. Remember the story of the young lady and her "100% supportive friends". There are also several mentoring programs and Master Mind groups available.

Some of the questions to ask yourself when considering a Master Mind group:

(1) What are the time and financial commitment, and other requirements to be a part of this group?

(2) Who else is in the Group? What are their businesses?

(3) What benefit are these members to me, and what benefit am I to them by participating in this group?

(4) Am I willing to keep ALL the required commitments?

(5) What do I expect to receive, achieve or accomplish from being in this group?

(d) If you said …
I don't know how it will be done or accomplished.

Very few people have all the answers when they set about *desiring* new things and conditions in their lives. Instead of thinking about how to do it, they focused on it already accomplished.

"Our minds become magnetized with the dominating thoughts we hold in our minds and these magnets attract to us the forces, the people, the circumstances of life which harmonize with the nature of our dominating thoughts."
~ Napoleon Hill ~

As you follow *The Plan* and *The Three Positive Rules of Accomplishment* you will be impregnating your mind with your *DESIRES*. The clearer you hold these pictures your mind you will find yourself drawing the people and circumstances to you that you need.

"You have to recognize when the right place and the right time fuse and take advantage of that opportunity. There are plenty of opportunities out there.
You can't sit back and wait."
~ Ellen Metcalf ~

(e) *If you said ...*
I don't have the time.

"Time is the coin of your life.
It is the only coin you have, and only you can
determine how it will be spent."
~ Carl Sandburg ~

If someone offered you all the money you *desired* if you would only get up 15 minutes earlier – would you?

If someone offered you the body you *desired* if you would give them 15 minutes of your lunch hour – would you?

If someone offered you what you *desired* most in life, if you would turn the TV off for 15 minutes at night – would you?

"How we spend our days is, of course,
how we spend our lives."
~ Annie Dillard ~

There are many excuses used by people. Only a few of them have been addressed. When you find yourself using one, ask yourself – how badly do I really *desire* what I say I *desire*?

"Struggle ends
where commitment begins." *
~ Sumner Davenport ~

*Voted to be included in the Top 10 Healthy Thoughts of 2007

3 Positive Rules of
Accomplishment - con't

The Omnipotent Power within you does not enter into any controversial argument. *It is waiting and willing to serve when you are ready,* but your objective mind is so susceptible to suggestion that it is almost impossible to make any satisfactory progress when surrounded by skeptics. Therefore, choose your friends carefully and associate with people who now have some of the thing you really *desire*, but *do not discuss your method of accomplishment with them.*

Put down on your *LIST* of *desire*s each material thing as money, home, automobile, or whatever it may be, but do not stop there. Be more definite. If you *desire* an automobile, decide *what kind, style, price, color,* and all the other details, including **when** you *desire* to have.

If you *desire* a home, plan the structure, grounds and furnishings decide on location and cost. If you *desire* money, write down the amount. If you *desire* to break a record in your business, put it down. It may be a sales record. If so, write out the total, the date requited, then the number of items you must sell to make it, also *LIST* your prospects and put after each name the sum expected. This may seem foolish at first, but you can never realize your desires if you do not *know positively and in detail what you desire and when you desire it.*

If you can not decide this, you are not serious.

 Re-read Simple Key DESIRE

You **must** be definite, and when you are, results will be surprising and almost unbelievable.

A natural and ancient enemy will no doubt appear when you get your first taste of accomplishment.

This enemy is Discredit, in form of such thoughts as: "It can't be possible; it just happened to be. What a remarkable coincidence!"

INSPIRED ACTION

When you keep the things you *desire*, the things on your *LIST*, in your mind, you will find your outward focus changes as well. You will begin to notice opportunities you may have missed or overlooked before. You will have flashes of inspiration that will give you ideas of things to do, and places to go.

Here's an area where many people choose to ignore their answers.

One example that may seem obvious is the person who claims to want to make a change in their body appearance. They complain that no matter what they do, they cannot lose weight. Yet they are consistently hearing the answer from within that they must make a commitment to change. They must make a consistent change in their eating habits or their exercise, or something else. Are you committing to the cookie in the moment or having the body you desire for a lifetime?

One person kept hearing the message that in order to drop the excess weight she must give up smoking cigarettes. Many of her well-meaning friends kept telling her that she would add more weight if she gave up smoking. Eventually she started listening to inspired guidance and stopped smoking. As she learned the new habit of breathing, she also saw her excess weight dissolve.

However, another example that may not seem so obvious would be the person who desires to have a loving, supportive and committed relationship, yet they continue to be with partners who treat them with disrespect. When they hear the guidance on how to be with the person they *say* they desire, they ignore the message and continue to behave the way they always have, and continue to attract and spend time with the same type of partners.

A person wanting to start a new business may hear the message that they should take the time to write a strategic business plan so they can see their path clearly from all views. Many want-to-be entrepreneurs have ignored this message, and continue to open and close businesses without reaching the level of success they originally desired. They continue to use old habits and attempt to create new results.

When you want new results in your life, you must be willing to listen to inspired guidance and your intuition in order to hear the answers to your questions. You must be willing to follow these messages and answers until they lead you to the next answer.

Each step on your journey is guided towards your desires, when you **listen and watch.**

Mindfulness is an essential part of this Key. Mindfulness is being fully present in each moment of your life and being aware in all your experiences. Mindfulness is listening to your inner voice, your body signals and using this information to consciously make your choices. Mindfulness is being aware of "why" you do the things you do and choosing to do the same or make conscious changes. Mindfulness is listening and paying attention to the answers, when you ask "How" can I have things different in my life? (You can learn more about Mindfulness in the RECOMMENDED READING section of this book)

Start the habit of carrying a small notepad with you at all times. As a faith building exercise, keep notes of these "coincidences" and "intuitions". In short time you will see that you are seeing and hearing answers that lead you closer to having what you wrote on your *LIST*.

As you consistently focus on your desires, you will discover articles, ideas, people and events suddenly appear in your line of sight and hearing. Many of these answers have already been in your life, yet you did not notice them or listen to them. Have you ever bought a new car, and afterwards, suddenly saw the same model or color seemingly everywhere? Did everyone go out and buy the same car as you, or are you now more aware of the other cars which were always there? The cars, just like your answers, have always been there; however, until you change your focus they were not recognized or considered significant.

You may experience inspiration and creative ideas that are very new to you. Write down all your ideas and inspiration.

When your mind is open is your most creative time. When you receive these "intuitive thoughts" and "coincidences", you will find the very answers that you seek to assist you to overcome your own obstacles.

When you write them into your notebook, you are emptying your mind and making space for more new ideas and inspiration.

"Sit down before fact as a little child,
be prepared to give up every preconceived
notion, follow humbly wherever
or whatever abysses nature leads, or
you will learn nothing."
~ Thomas H. Huxley ~

As you receive these creative ideas and answers it is important to take action on them right away. Even when the action is to "stop and listen". One answer or clue may lead you to another, and another. One person you talk to may lead you to another. One dedicated and inspired action you take may lead you to several more.

There are those who would like to believe that all they need to do is think about what they *desire* and it "magically" appears. The truth is: Some form of **action is required.**

"Knowing is not enough;

we must apply!"

~ Goethe ~

A joke is told about man who wrote on his *LIST* that he *wanted* to win the Lottery. Every day he looked at his *LIST*; he also prayed to God for it. This went on for days, and no one knocked at his door to tell him he had won the lottery. One day he changed his prayer to "Why haven't you given me what I have on my LIST? Why haven't I won the Lottery?

A booming voice came back with a question of its own: "*Have you at least bought a ticket?!*"

3 Positive Rules of
Accomplishment - con't

When such thoughts occur, *give thanks and assert credit to your Omnipotent Power* for this accomplishment. By doing this, you gain assurance and more accomplishment, and in time, prove to yourself that *there is a law, which actually works – at all times* - when you are in tune with it.

Sincere and serious thanks can not be given without gratitude and it is impossible to be thankful and grateful without being happy.

Therefore, when you are thanking your greatest and best friend, *your Omnipotent Power,* for the gifts received, do so *with all your soul, and let it be reflected in your face.*

The Power and what it does is beyond understanding. Do not try to understand it, but *accept the accomplishment* with thankfulness, happiness and strengthened faith.

GRATITUDE

The Most Important Key to Everything is GRATITUDE!

Some people say "I'll be grateful when *(fill in the blank)* happens, or I get *(fill in the blank)*, or when this *(fill in the blank)* does what I want....."

This is one sure way to continue struggling for what you wrote on your *LIST*.

Step #1:

Start a Gratitude *LIST* right now!

(a) What are you grateful for in your life right now? **Write it down.**

Before going any farther in this book, or doing anything else, write down what are grateful for, right now in your day and your life.

Start Here:

Simple Key - GRATITUDE

Step 2:

Start a Gratitude **BOOK.**

(a) Take those photos that you have been collecting of those places you have visited; the people you had fun with; the things you have done; the activities you participated in and enjoyed; and take them out of hiding and put them in a beautiful "Gratitude Book".

(b) Next to each photo on the page write notes why you are grateful for the experience, the people, etc.

(c) Label the front of your Binder as YOUR Gratitude Book. Put your name on it.

If you find a photo that brings up feelings other than gratitude and joy – GET RID OF IT! What positive reason do you have to hold onto it? Keep only reminders of what you are Grateful for and you will find yourself with more to be Grateful for.

Step #3:

When you start your Mindful Meditation or prayer focus on your DESIRES, begin with thoughts and images of what you are grateful for. Take the emotions of Gratitude into your focus on your DESIRES.

Step #4:

Before going to sleep each night, write three (3) things that you are Grateful for from your day. Keep adding to your list. You may find yourself repeating some of the same things, and that is good.

Make a commitment that even on those days when you are tired and maybe the day didn't exactly end up the way you had hoped, you will still find a minimum of three things to be Grateful for and write in your book.

START RIGHT NOW looking at your life with Gratitude.

CAUTION

It is possible to desire and obtain that which will make you miserable; that which will wreck the happiness of yourself or others; that which will cause sickness and death; that which will rob you of eternal life.

You can have what you *desire*, but you must take all that goes with it; so in planning your *desires*, *plan that which you are sure will give to you and your fellow people, the greatest good here on earth; thus paving the way to that future hope beyond the scope of human understanding.*

This method of securing what you *desire* applies to everything you are capable of *desiring* and the scope being so great, it is suggested that your first *LIST* consist of only those things with which you are quite familiar, such as an amount of money or accomplishments, or the possession of material things. Such *desires* as these are more easily and quickly obtained than the discontinuance of fixed habits, the welfare of others and the healing of mental or bodily ills.

Accomplish the lesser things first. Then take the next step, and when that is accomplished, you will see the higher and really important objectives in life, but long before you reach this state of your progress, many worth while *desires* will find their place on your *LIST*.

One will be to help others as you have been helped. *Great is the reward to those who help and give without thought of self, as it is impossible to be unselfish without gain.*

IN CONCLUSION

A short while ago, Dr. Emil Coue came to this country and showed thousands of people how to help themselves. Thousands of others spoofed at the idea, refused his assistance and are today where they were before his visit.

So with the statements and plan presented to you now, you can reject or accept.

You can remain as you are or *have anything you desire.*

The choice is yours.

But God grant that you may find in this short volume the inspiration to choose aright, follow the plan and thereby obtain, as so many others have, all things, whatever, they may be, that you desire.

Read the entire book *over again, and again, AND THEN AGAIN.*

Memorize the three simple rules.

Test them now on what you desire this minute. Start your list here:

RESULTS

Your results speak for themselves.

"Let my efforts be known by their results."

~ Emily Brontë ~

If you already have everything you desire, then continue what you are now doing.

On the other hand, if you are still meeting with disappointments and frustrations then re-read this book, and follow the techniques - with commitment and consistent effort – and embrace your new results. This is where the "rich get richer" cliché comes into play.

As you commit to changing your thoughts, your actions and habits, you will attract new people, new things and new results.

The MASTER KEY to your success with the message presented in this book is your commitment to taking **consistent** action.

As you begin to see new results in your life, you may attract people who want to know how you did it. You will then be able to speak from experience and assist others. You will also attract people to you who recognize your commitments and will offer more answers to assist you.

TESTIMONIAL: "I wrote my list in specific detail.
I got everything I had written on my list – and more!
I got bonuses!" Mor Koren, Los Angeles, CA

The 3rd Edition of this book will be published with testimonials from readers who applied the tools and the results they saw. If you would like to submit your testimonial for consideration for inclusion in the 3rd Edition, please email to:

info@selfinvestmentpublishing.com.

Be sure to indicate "It Works With simple Keys Testimonial" in the subject line.

FREQUENTLY ASKED
QUESTIONS

Q: *Is this really necessary? Are these techniques really done by successful people?*

A: You have read previously in this book about Jim Carey, Chicken Soup for the Soul and other familiar names, and the results they produced.

These techniques are used by people planning a party or a vacation. They write a list. They read their list consistently. They add to and subtract from their list. They "see" their end result in advance and they follow their "inspired thoughts" to make the party or vacation a success.

Many people do the same in planning their lives so consistently that it becomes a part of them, felt as second nature. They then naturally begin each goal or desire with a vision and a list and they think about the end result **consistently**. They think in the possible rather than the impossible; they follow the inspired guidance, sometimes referred to as intuition and continue this effort until their dream is realized. When you do the same, you will find **It Works**.

Q: *I get discouraged when the results aren't what I wanted. Now what?*

A: When this happens, many people will mistakenly think they are doing something wrong, or they can't have what they are asking for or other destructive thoughts. Every result either takes you directly closer to your DESIRES, or it has an answer for your next step.

 See Simple Key – FRUSTRATION BUMP

Q: *How long does this process take before I get what I desire?*

A: There is no way for me to measure how long or how quickly your desires will show up in your life. The control is yours. The speed of your results will be in proportion to your beliefs, your commitment to having your desires, your conscious awareness of your focus and your thoughts, plus your consistent follow through when you receive inspiration.

> *"You are given the gifts of the gods,*
> *you create your reality*
> *according to you beliefs.*
> *Yours is the creative energy*
> *that makes your world.*
> *There are no limitations to the self*
> *except those you believe in."*
> *~ Seth ~*

It Works with Simple Keys

Quote References

William Arthur Ward

(1921 – 1994)

One of America's most quoted writers of inspirational maxims. More than 100 articles, poems and meditations written by Ward have been published in such magazines as Reader's Digest, This Week, The Upper Room, Together, The Christian Advocate, The Adult Student, The Adult Teacher, The Christian Home, The Phi Delta Kappan, Science of Mind, The Methodist Layman, Sunshine, and Ideals. His column Pertinent Proverbs has been featured in numerous service club publications throughout the United States and abroad.

James Gordon, M.D

Gordon is the Founder and Director of the Center for Mind-Body Medicine in Washington, DC and is a Clinical Professor in the Departments of Psychiatry and Family Medicine at the Georgetown University School of Medicine. Dr. Gordon recently served as Chairman of the White House Commission on Complementary and Alternative Medicine Policy.

Robert Holden

An Author & Psychologist who has written several books including 'Shift Happens! He is Director of The Happiness Project - a pioneer in the field of positive psychology and well-being. (www.happiness.co.uk)

BYRON

(1788-1824)

Byron was among the most famous of the English 'Romantic' poets, and personality captured the imagination of Europe.

Doris Lessing

(1919-)

A British writer, author of several acclaimed works.

Lessing won the Nobel Prize in Literature. Lessing is the eleventh woman to win the prize in its 106-year history, and also the oldest person ever to win the literature award.

Helen Keller

(1880-1968)

Keller became deaf and blind after a serious illness at age 19 months. She went on to accomplish great things in the "seeing and hearing" world. Through her writings, lectures and the way she lived her life, she has shown millions of people that disability need not be the end of the world.

George Bernard Shaw

(1856-1950)

Shaw wrote more than sixty plays and is known to have written more than 250,000 letters. He is the only person to have been awarded both a Nobel Prize (the Nobel Prize in Literature in 1925) and an Oscar (Academy Award for Writing Adapted Screenplay in 1939 for Pygmalion). He was a strong advocate for socialism and women's rights, a vegetarian and teetotaller.

Margaret Laurence

(1926-1987)

A well published author whose early novels were influenced by her experience as a minority in Africa.

They show a strong sense of Christian symbolism and ethical concern for being a white person in a colonial state. She wrote The Stone Angel, the book for which she is best known. Published in 1964, the novel is of the literary form that looks at the entire life of a person.

Walt Whitman

(1819-1892)

Whitman was proclaimed the "greatest of all American poets" by many foreign observers a mere four years after his death; he is viewed as the first urban poet. His works have even been translated into more than 25 languages.

Shankaracharya

Shankaracharya is a commonly used title of heads of maṭhas (monasteries) in the Advaita tradition. The title derives from Śankara of Kaladi, a theologian of Hinduism, who established four maṭhas in the four regions of India.

Win Ng

(1936-1991)

A renowned ceramicist and craftsman. A native of San Francisco's Chinatown and a graduate of the San Francisco Art Institute, Win Ng was among a key group of post World War II artists responsible for establishing a new tradition of American pottery. Win Ng also established himself as a consummate decorative designer and innovative entrepreneur.

Martin Luther King, Jr.

(1929-1968)

King was the most famous leader of the American civil rights movement, a political activist, a Baptist minister, and was one of America's greatest orators. In 1964, King became the youngest man to be awarded the Nobel Peace Prize (for his work as a peacemaker, promoting nonviolence and equal treatment for different races). In 1968, King was assassinated. He was posthumously awarded the Presidential Medal of Freedom the Congressional Gold Medal. In 1986, Martin Luther King Day was established as a United States holiday. His most influential and well-known public address is the "I Have a Dream" speech.

Mother Teresa
(1910 – 1997)

Mother Teresa was an Albanian Roman Catholic nun who founded the Missionaries of Charity and won the Nobel Peace Prize in 1979 for her humanitarian work. For over forty years she ministered to the poor, sick, orphaned, and dying in Kolkata (Calcutta), India. By the 1970s she had become internationally famed as a humanitarian and advocate for the poor and helpless. Following her death she was beatified by Pope John Paul II and given the title Blessed Teresa of Calcutta.

Richard Cecil
(1748- 1810)

Cecil was a leading Evangelical Anglican clergyman of the 18th and 19th centuries.

Samuel Johnson LL.D.

(1709 –1784),

Often referred to simply as Dr Johnson, one of England's greatest literary figures: a poet, essayist, biographer and lexicographer, often considered the finest critic of English literature. He was also a great wit and prose stylist whose bons mots are still frequently quoted in print today.

Les Brown

Successful Entrepreneur, Best Selling Author, Radio and Television Celebrity. www.lesbrown.com

Epictetus

(Greek: c.55–c.135)

A Greek Stoic philosopher. He lived most of his life in Rome until his exile to northwestern Greece, with other philosophers by the emperor Domitian. This began what would later come to be the most celebrated part of his life. After his exile, Epictetus founded a famed philosophical school. This school was even visited by Emperor Hadrian, and its most famous student, Arrian, became a great historian in his own right.   The name given by his parents, if one was given, is not known - the word epiktetos in Greek simply means "acquired." Epictetus spent his youth productively, studying Stoic Philosophy under Musonius Rufus. One of his teachings "The Manual" is available through Self-Investment Company-Publishing Division.

Malcolm Stevenson Forbes

(1919 –1990)

Publisher of Forbes magazine founded by his father B.C. Forbes. Malcolm Forbes was legendary for his lavish lifestyle which he could amply afford with his abundant financial successes.

Thomas Edison

(1847-1931)

Edison is considered one of the most prolific inventors in history, holding 1,093 U.S. patents in his name, as well as many patents in the United Kingdom, France and Germany. Edison's greatest contribution was the first practical electric lighting. He not only invented the first successful electric light bulb, but also set up the first electrical power distribution company. Edison invented the phonograph, and made improvements to the telegraph, telephone and motion picture technology. He also founded the first modern research laboratory.

Napoleon Hill

(1883-1970)

An American author was one of the earliest producers of the modern genre of personal-success literature. His most famous work, *Think and Grow Rich*, is the all time bestseller in the field. In America, Hill stated in his writings, people are free to believe what they want to believe, and this is what sets the United States apart from all other countries in the world. Hill's works examined the power of personal beliefs, and the role they play in personal success. "What the mind of man can conceive and believe, it can achieve" is one of Hill's hallmark expressions.

Dave Thomas

(1932-2002)

American Entrepreneur/businessman, founder of Wendy's restaurants.

Ellen Metcalf

Ms. Metcalf's quote is motivating and quoted often. Any information on her personally, her works and accomplishments would be appreciated. Please send to : books@selfinvestmentpublishing.com.

Carl Sandburg

(1878-1967)

A successful journalist, poet, historian, biographer and autobiographer. During the course of his career, Sandburg won two Pulitzer Prizes, one for his biography of Abraham Lincoln (*Abraham Lincoln: The War Years*) and one for his collection *The Complete Poems of Carl Sandburg*.

Annie Dillard

An American author. She won the Pulitzer Prize for *Tinker Creek*. She is also well known for her memoir about growing up in Pittsburgh, *An American Childhood*. Dillard also wrote an essay called *The Deer at Providencia* and the book "*Teaching a Stone to Talk*". She has an ongoing quest for knowledge, often reading over 100 books a year.

Sumner Davenport

(1951-)

Co-author and Editor of this book.

A real life example of an impassioned visionary, Sumner M. Davenport began her career at age nine when she opened her first lemonade stand and a backyard carnival. Throughout her childhood she was inspired by the successful business people she saw. She used this early education as a foundation when she started her first of many unique and interesting entrepreneurial ventures at age 19. Sumner is a woman with a unquenchable thirst for knowing the answers to life. Her inquisitiveness began as a child. Her deepest passion is to see people empowering others while living the life of their dreams. She encourages others to question their premature cognitive commitments and discover their own truth. Sumner is the recipient of several awards and acknowledgements. She credits her best education to The University of Hard Knocks, with crash courses in taking risks and advanced learning from bouncing back. For several years Sumner has stood up for Self Investment rather than self-improvement. Throughout the twists, turns and painful bumps in her life, she has rebuilt her self-esteem by reminding herself that who she is, is not who other people judge her to be, nor their acceptance of her. People are attracted to Sumner for her willingness to share the secrets to her own success. She facilitates meditation groups and coaches others who are experiencing bumps in their journey. Her focus is "Self awareness, understanding and personal evolvement not self improvement." She is sought after as a speaker on several life experience, spiritual and business topics. She has co-authored several books to include some of her examples of how to triumph over life challenges and she is quoted often. One of Sumner's quotes was voted to be included in the Top 10 Healthy Thoughts of 2007. She can be reached through her website: www.sumnerdavenport.com

Albert Einstein

(1879-1955)

German-born theoretical physicist, best known for his theory of relativity and specifically mass-energy equivalence, $E = mc2$. Einstein received the 1921 Nobel

Prize in Physics; In 1999 Einstein was named Time magazine's "Person of the Century", and a poll of prominent physicists named him the greatest physicist of all time. Today, the name "Einstein" has become synonymous with genius.

Henry David Thoreau

(1817-1862)

An American author, poet and philosopher, a complex man of many talents who worked hard to shape his craft and his life, seeing little difference between them. Among his lasting contributions were his writings on natural history and philosophy, where he anticipated the methods and findings of ecology and environmental history, two sources of modern day environmentalism.

Shinichi Suzuki

(1898-1998)

Through his special method of teaching music, Dr. Suzuki showed teachers and parents everywhere what children could do. He also believed that hearing and playing great music helped children become good people with beautiful, peaceful hearts. He lived to be 99 years old, and he always seemed young, full of energy, cheerful and loving.

MIRACLE CARTOON
Copyright Sydney Harris
http://sciencecartoonsplus.com/
Reprinted with permission

Carl Jung
(1875-1961)
A Swiss psychiatrist, influential man and founder of analytical psychology. His unique and broadly influential approach to psychology emphasized understanding the psyche through exploring the worlds of dreams, art, mythology, world religion and philosophy.

Charles A. Garfield
The author of the widely acclaimed "Peak Performance" trilogy: *Peak Performers*, *Team Management*, and *Second to None*

Bhagavad Gita
Song of God" is an ancient Sanskrit text comprising 700 verses from the *Bhishma Parva* of the Mahabharata and

is well known of all the sacred scriptures from ancient
India.

Doug King

President and Chief Executive Officer of the St. Louis
Science Center. He leads a team of 250 staff members
and 500 volunteers whose mission is to stimulate
interest in and an understanding of science and
technology.

T.E. Lawrence

(1888-1935)

Popularly known as Lawrence of Arabia, Lawrence
became famous for his exploits as British Military liaison
to the Arab Revolt during the First World War.
Lawrence's life and his book *The Seven Pillars of
Wisdom* formed the basis of David Lean's film, *Lawrence
of Arabia.*

Bryce Courtenay

Australia's top selling novelist with titles such as The
Power of One which is translated into eleven languages
and the subject of a major movie of the same name He

has lectured on the power of the individual to achieve any end purpose. He has been awarded The Order of Australia AM and the honorary degree of Doctor of Letters.

Thomas H. Huxley

(1825-1895)

Thomas Henry Huxley was one of the first adherents to Darwin's theory of evolution by natural selection, and did more than anyone else to advance its acceptance among scientists and the public alike.

Goethe

(1749–1832)

German poet, dramatist, novelist, and scientist. One of the great masters of world literature, his genius embraced most fields of human endeavor; his art and thought are epitomized in his great dramatic poem Faust. Goethe knew French, English, Italian, Latin, Greek, and Hebrew and translated works by Diderot, Voltaire, Cellini, Byron, and others. His approach to science was one of sensuous experience and poetic intuition.

Henry Ford

(1863- 1947)

Founder of the Ford Motor Company and father of modern assembly lines used in mass production. Although Ford was not the first to build a self-propelled vehicle with a gasoline engine, he was, however, one of several automotive pioneers who helped this country become a nation of motorists.

Seth

Spiritual messenger channeled by Jane Roberts. Seth's message through Jane Roberts consistently reported as saying: 1.) we create our own reality; 2.) our point of power is the present; 3.) we are not at the mercy of the subconscious, nor are we helpless; and 4.) We are gods couched in creature hood.

Emily Jane Brontë

(1818-1848)

A British novelist and poet, now best remembered for her novel Wuthering Heights, a classic of English literature. To evade contemporary prejudice against

female writers, she published under the masculine pen
name Ellis Bell.

RECOMMENDED READING

There are many teachers and tools to assist you in living the life of your dreams. We all learn from different teachers and different delivery of the message.

The following is a short list of books and authors which may assist you in finding your answers:

How to Turn Your Desires and Ideals Into Reality -
    Brown Landone, Foreword by Sumner M. Davenport
The "G" Spot, The ecstasy of life through Gratitude –
    Sumner M. Davenport
The Miracle of Mindfulness – Thich Nhat Hahn
Think and Grow Rich – Napoleon Hill
Practicing The Power of Now – Eckhart Tolle
The Hidden Messages in Water –Masaru Emoto
The Greatest Salesman in the World – Og Mandino
An Essay on Concentration – Ralph Waldo Emerson
Power vs. Force: The Hidden Determination of
    Human Behavior – David R. Hawkins
A Separate Reality – Carlos Castaneda

Radical Forgiveness – Colin Tipping

Illusions, the Adventures of a Reluctant Messiah

    – Richard Bach

No Ordinary Moments – Dan Millman

The Celestine Prophecy: An experimental Guide

    – James Redfield & Carol Adreinne

The Fantasy Bond – Robert W. Firestone, Ph.D.

The Body Reveals – Ron Kurtz & Hector Prestera, M.D.

Spirit at Work, Discovering the Spirituality in

    Leadership – Jay Conger & Associates

Synchronicity, the Inner Path of Leadership –

    Joseph Jaworski

Dhammapada, the Sayings of the Buddha

Creating true Prosperity – Shakti Gawain

Motivation & Personality – Abraham H. Maslow

The Law of Psychic Phenomena

    – Thomas J. Hudson, PhD

These and many other recommendations can be ordered through our websites:

www.selfinvestmentpublishing.com
http://astore.amazon.com/selfinvestment-20

Simple Keys

There are many authors and educators delivering the message of acquiring your desires. Many great motivators can get you "fired up" and ready to go, however what seems to be missing is some of the necessary action steps needed, or tools to assist you in getting over the "bumps in the road".

The Simple Keys teachings were introduced to fill that need. There are numerous "keys' to support your ongoing growth and assist you in the manifestation of your desires. This book presents only seven.

From a recent class participant: *"I now have a*

system that feels fabulous and fits into my everyday life. All the choices are yours. You are in control!!! It does not get much better than that."

Please visit our website for more information:
www.simplekeys.org

Self Investment Company, LLC

Self *Improvement* is %$#@!

*The **INVESTMENTS** we make in ourselves,*
always deliver the most profitable returns.™.

Our mission is to offer products and services that empower people by reminding them of their value and their capabilities. We choose to embrace the idea of Self Investment rather than self improvement.

Most people are doing the best they are capable of, with what they know and what they have to work with every day.

By saying a person needs to improve something suggests that they are wrong, are incomplete or imperfect by someone else's standards, A great deal of guilt and damage is made to a person's self esteem when they believe they are not as successful, as beautiful, as wealthy, as (fill in the blank) as someone else. There is a great amount of media and marketing that suggest a product, a look, a job or *(fill in the blank)* will improve a person.

We believe that the choices we make in our personal and professional life are based on the information we have at the moment, our premature cognitive commitments, our experiences, our education, our fears and other reactions.

When we invest in ourselves we are the best we are - every day.

Please visit our website for more information:
www.selfinvestment.com

We wish you more joyous abundance than you have ever experienced, realized, imagined or believed possible previously in your life.

SELF INVESTMENT COMPANY

SELF-INVESTMENT COMPANY © 2007
2219 E. Thousand Oaks Blvd. #102-386
Thousand Oaks, CA 91362

It Works with Simple Keys